# Hedgehogs Adult Coloring Book

***This book belongs to:***

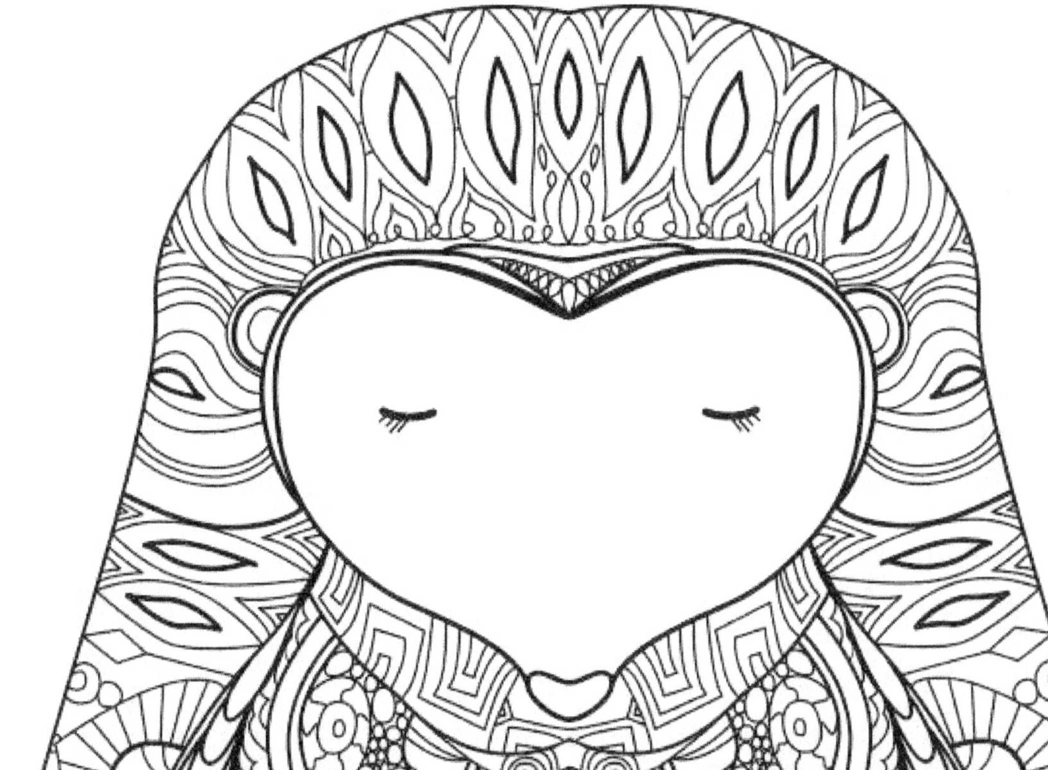

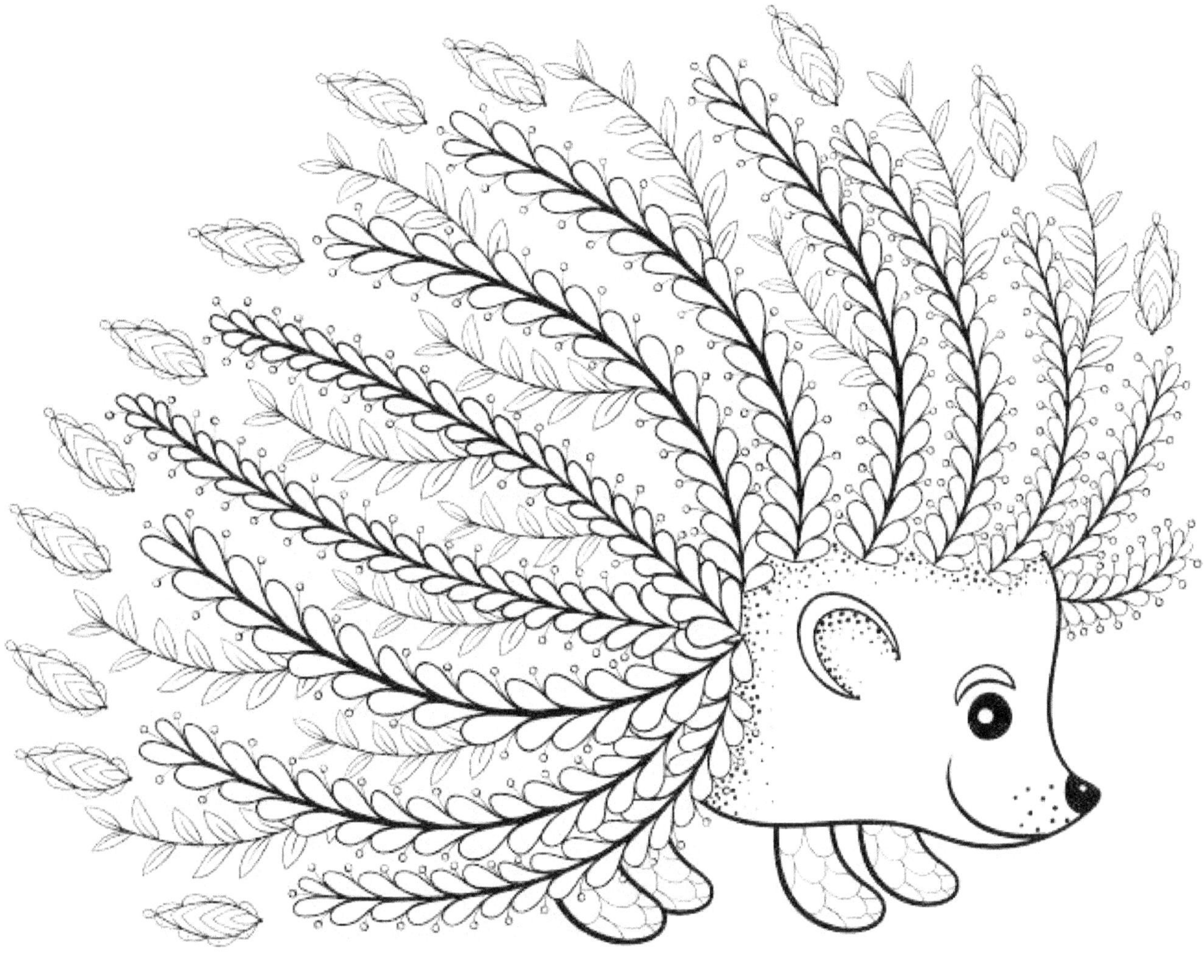

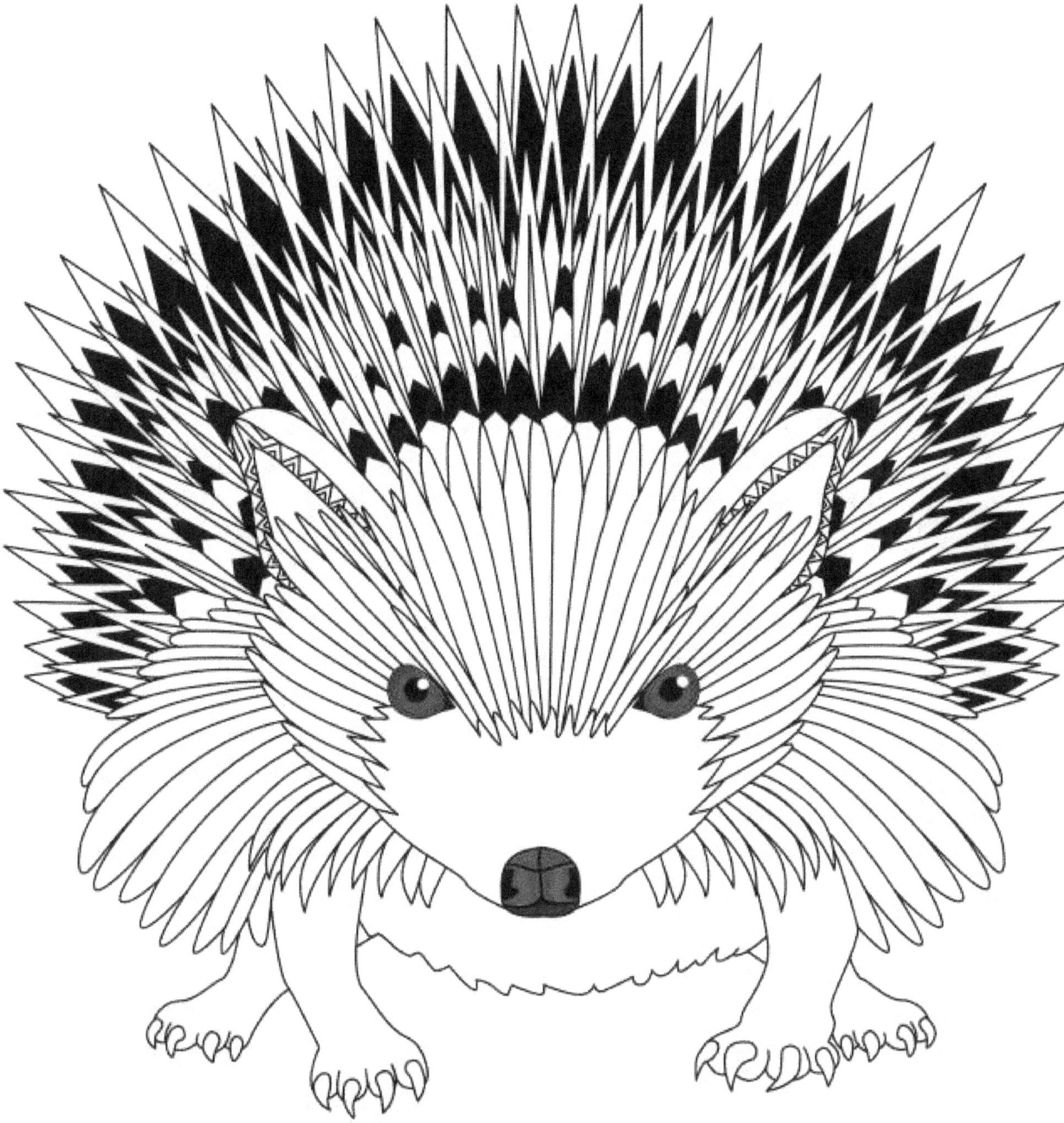

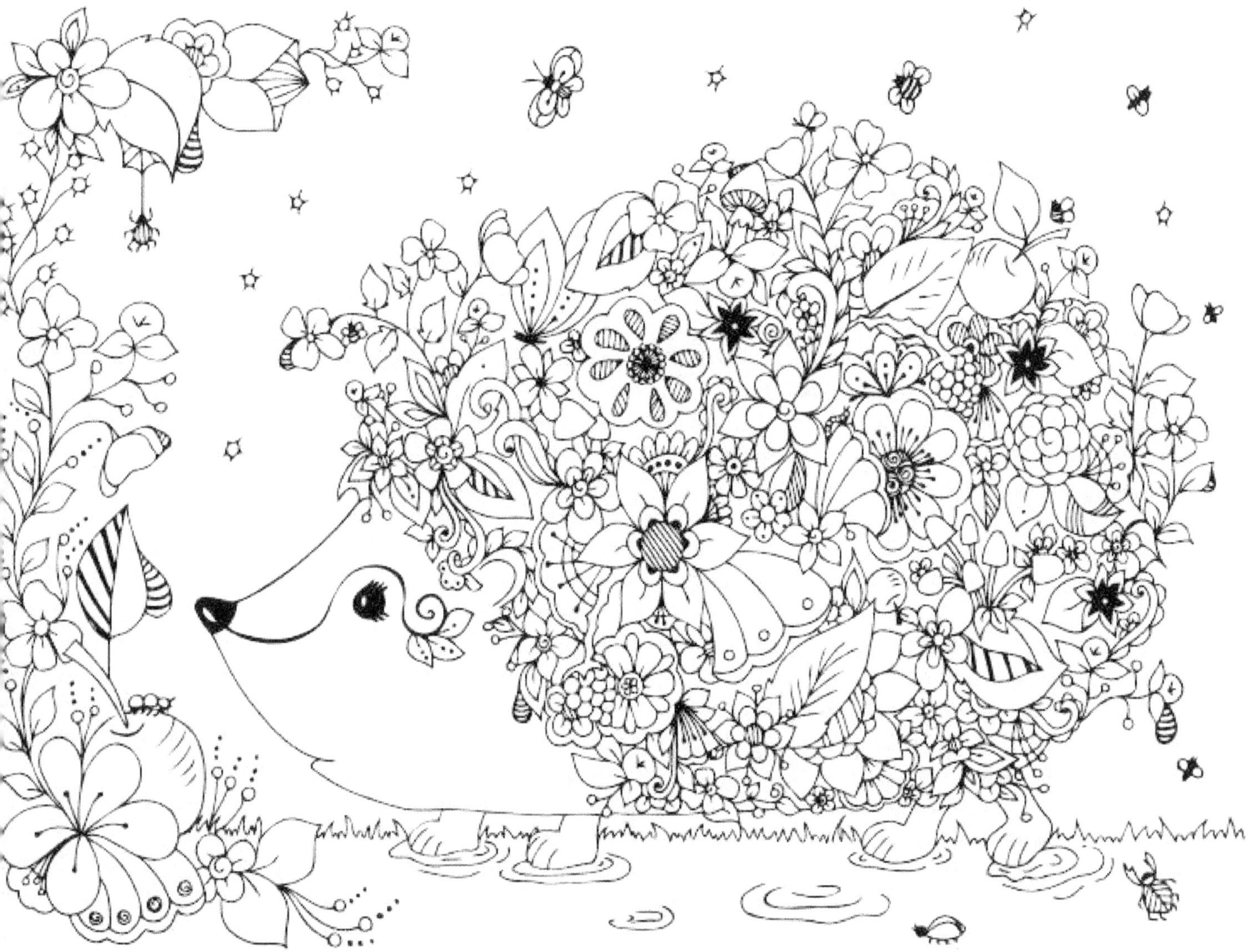

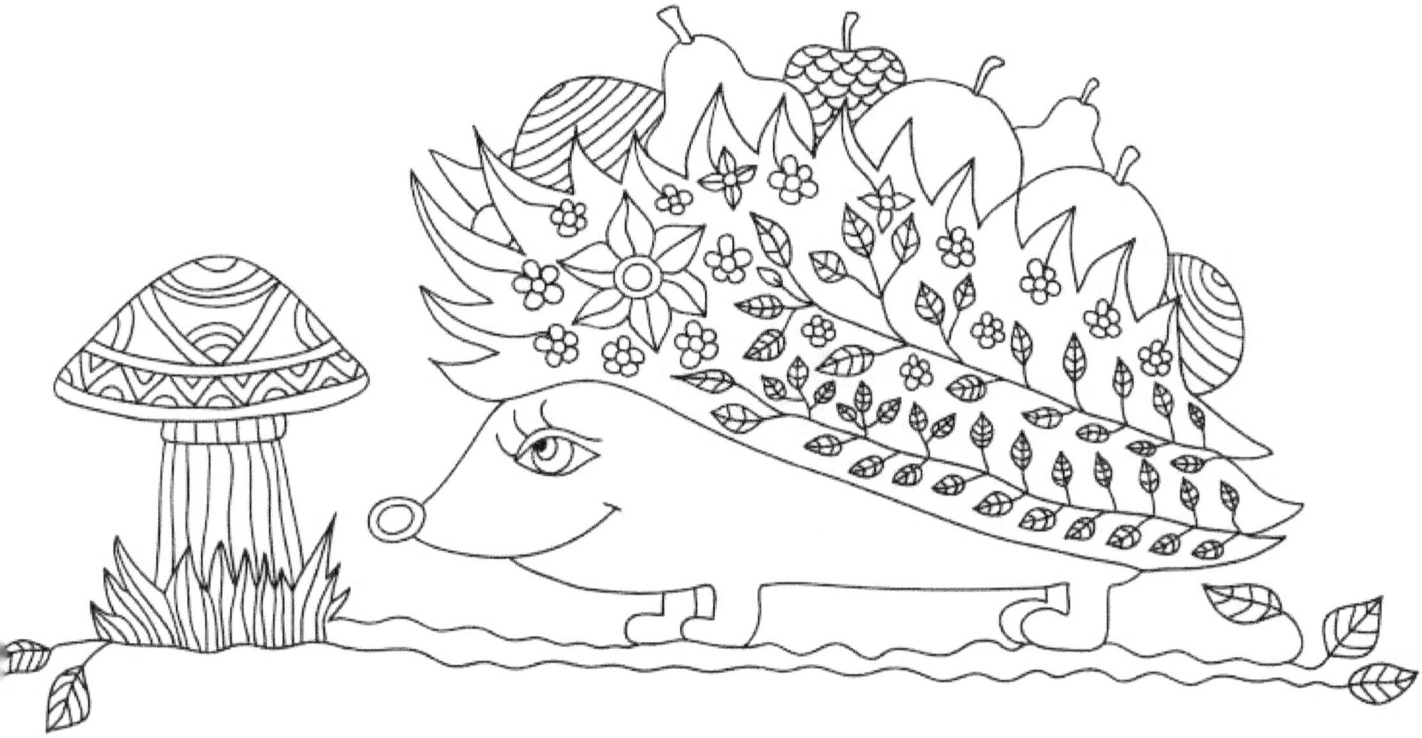

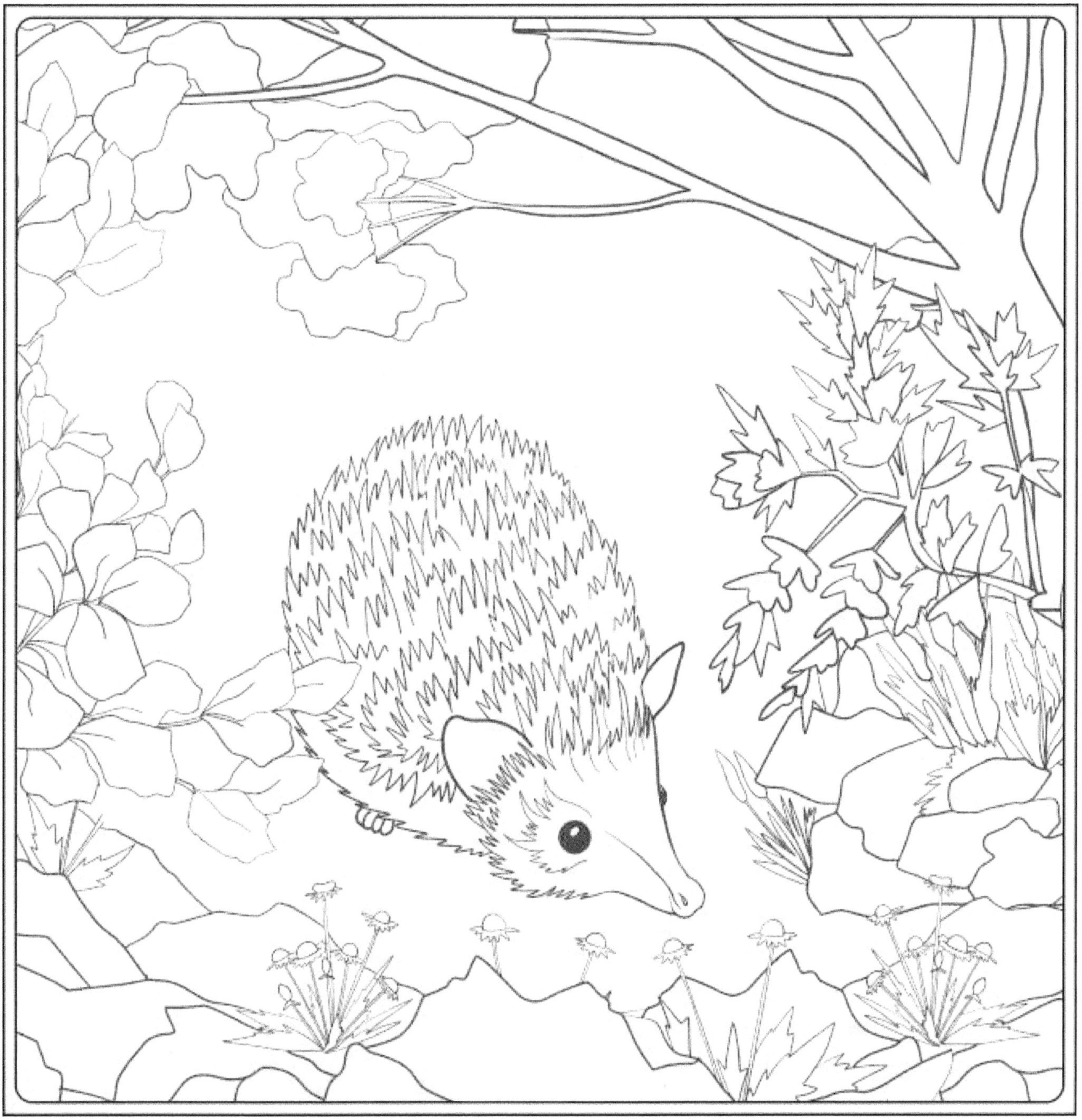

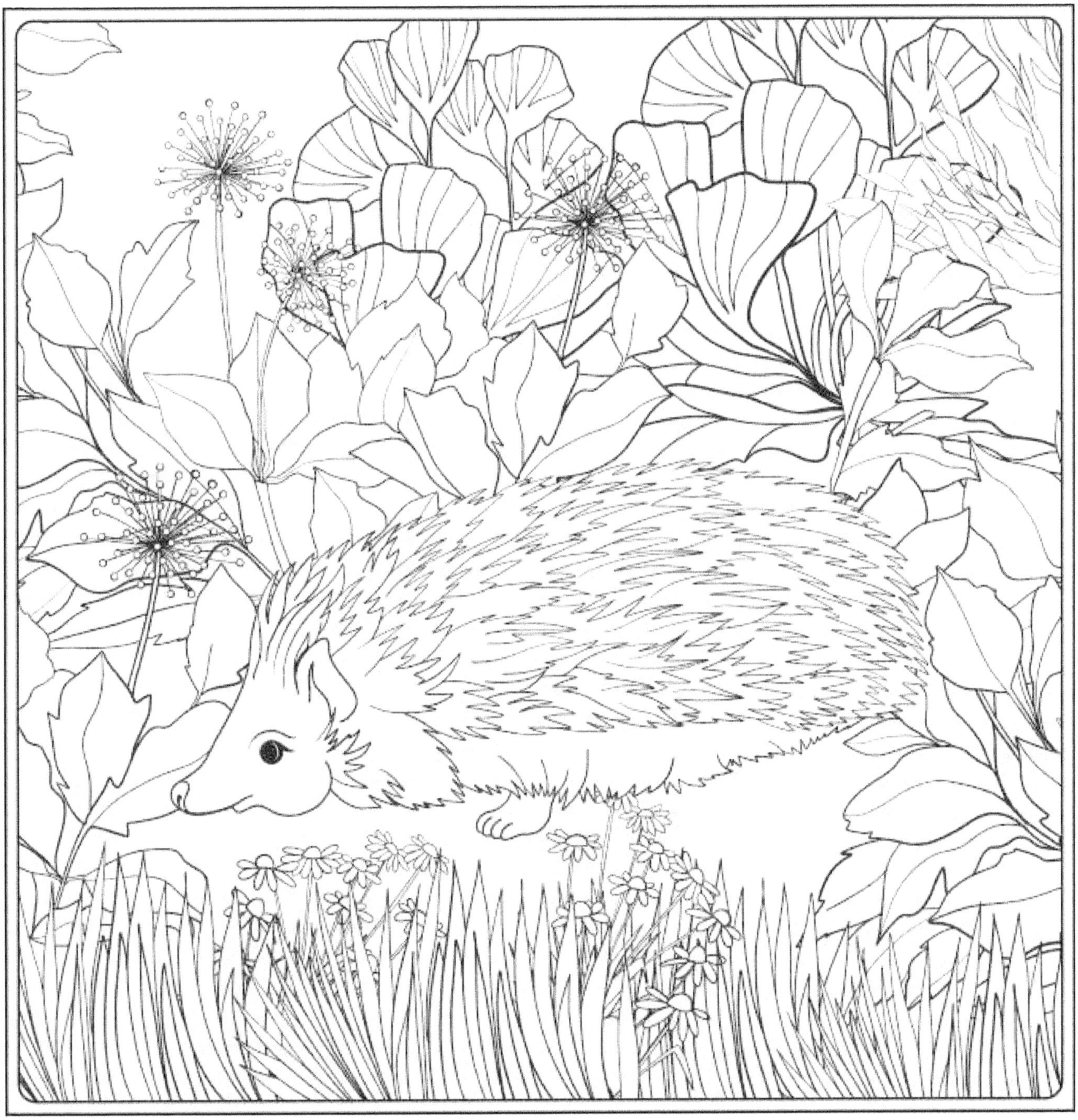

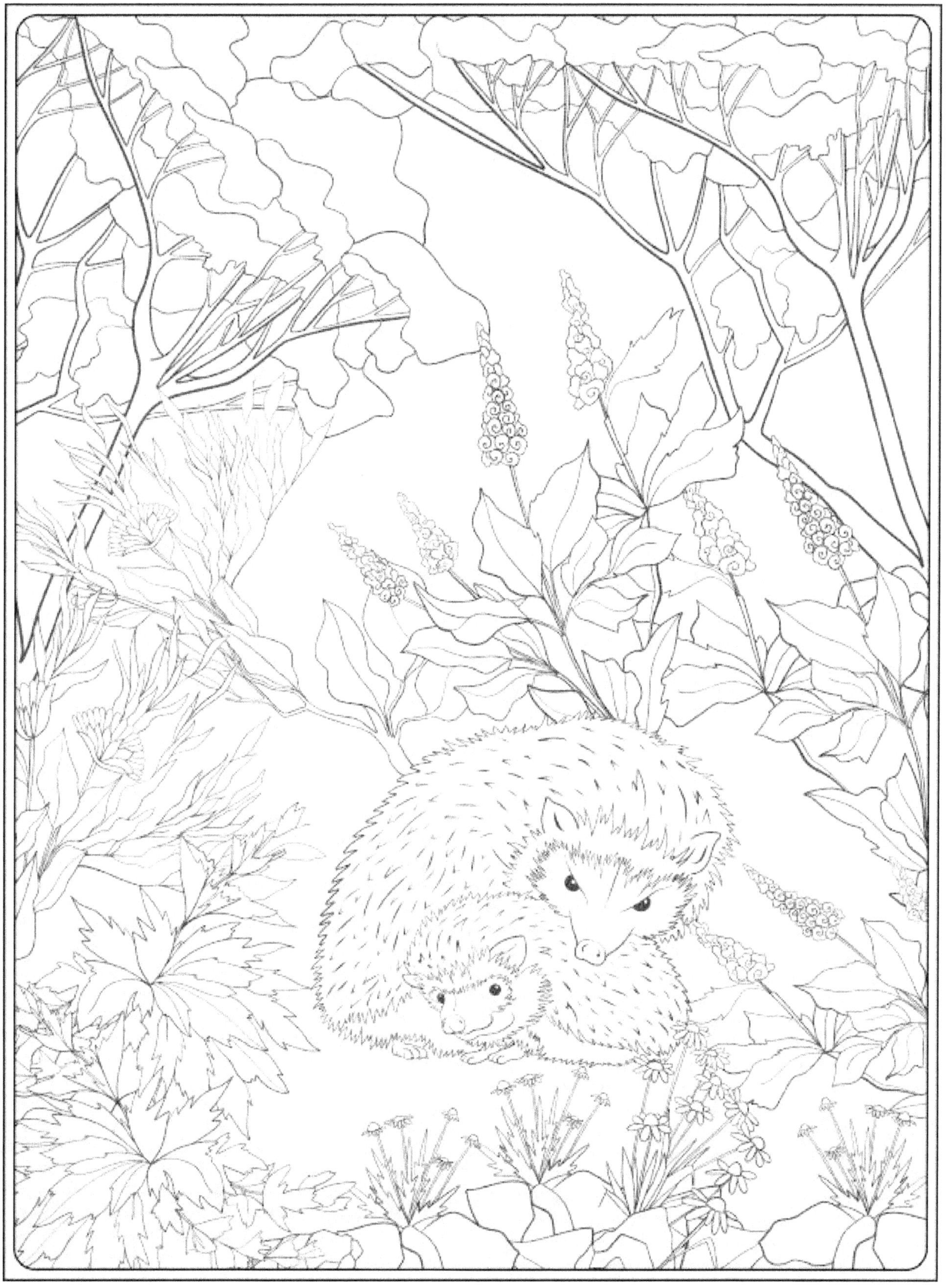

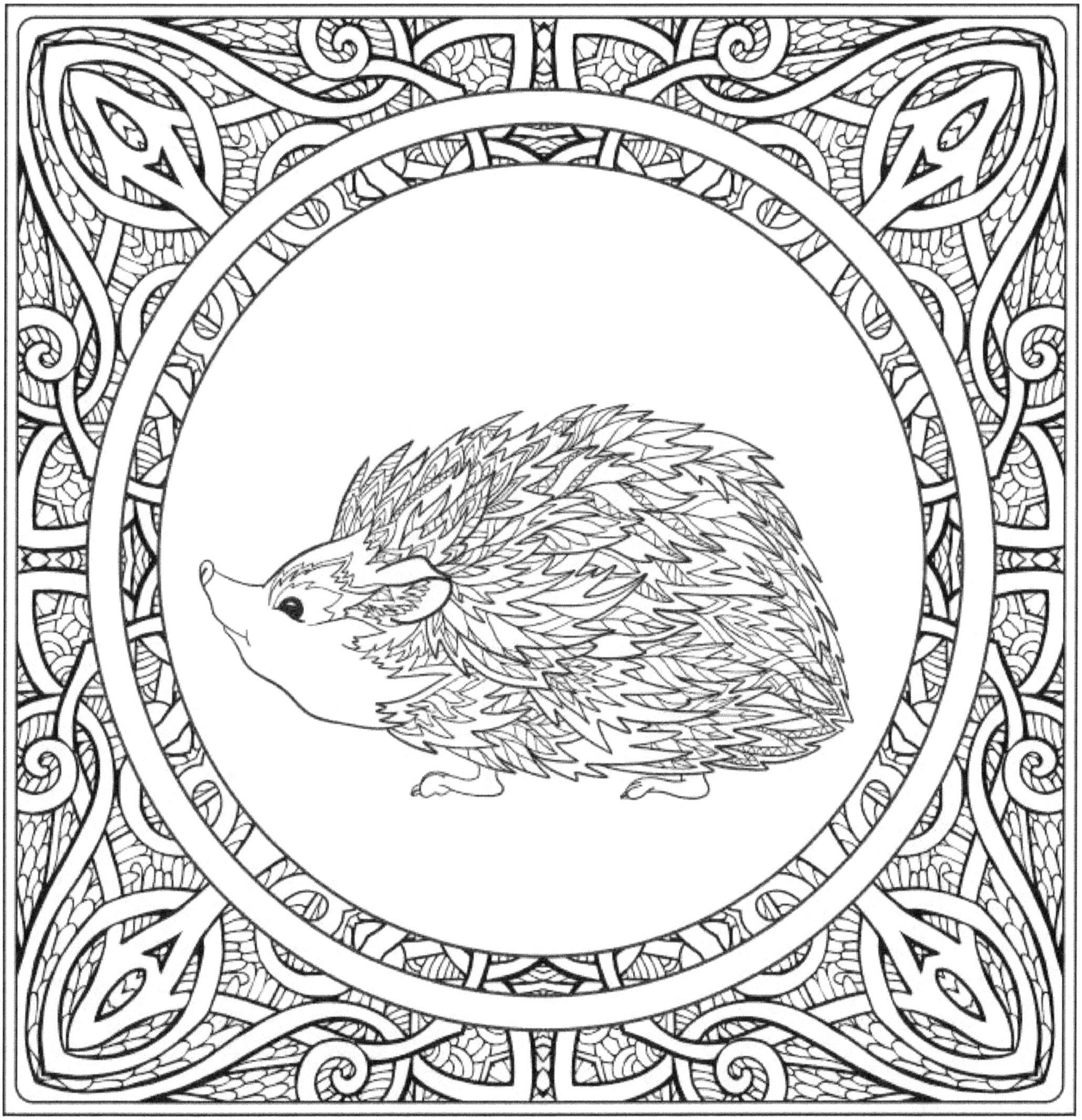

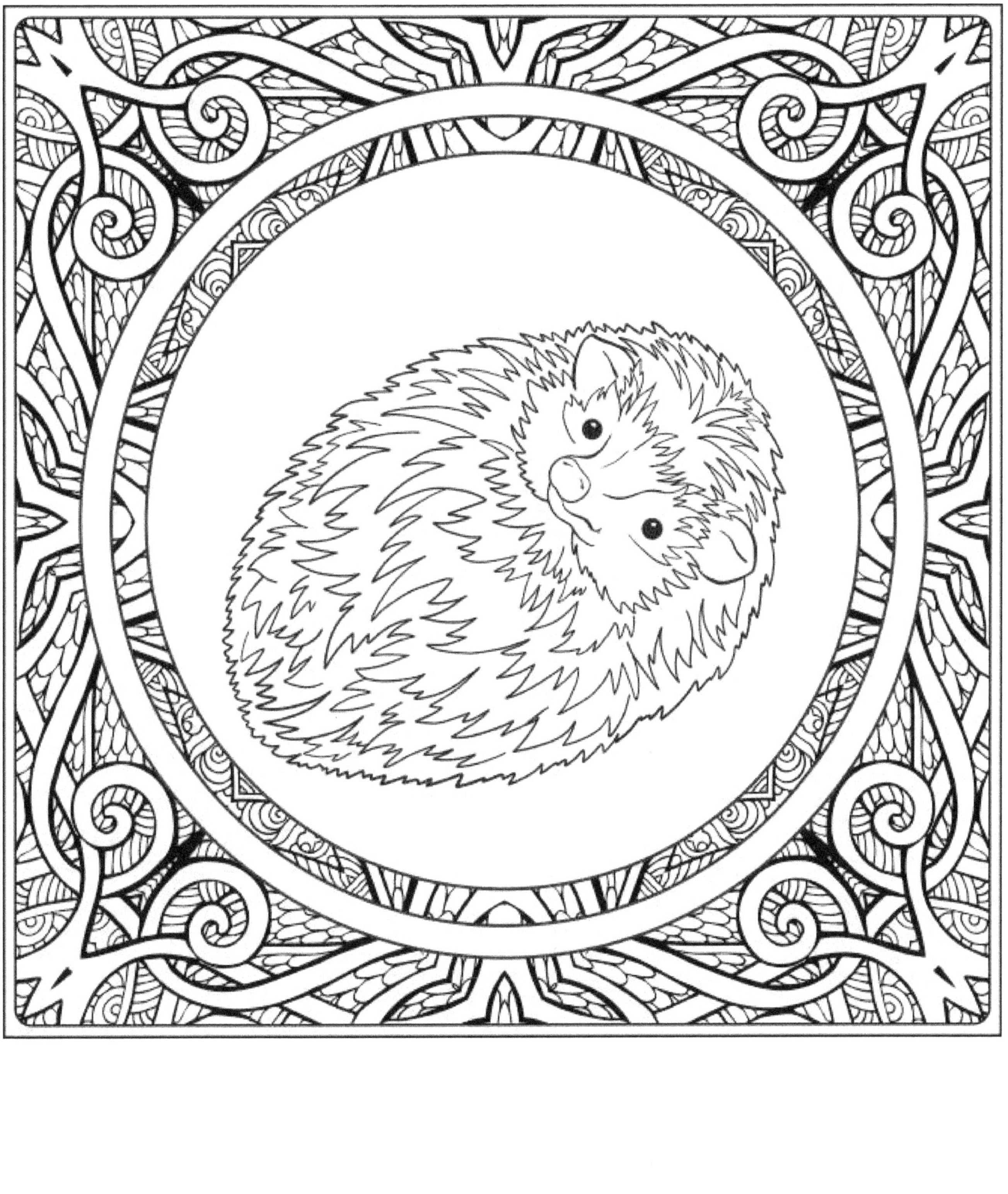

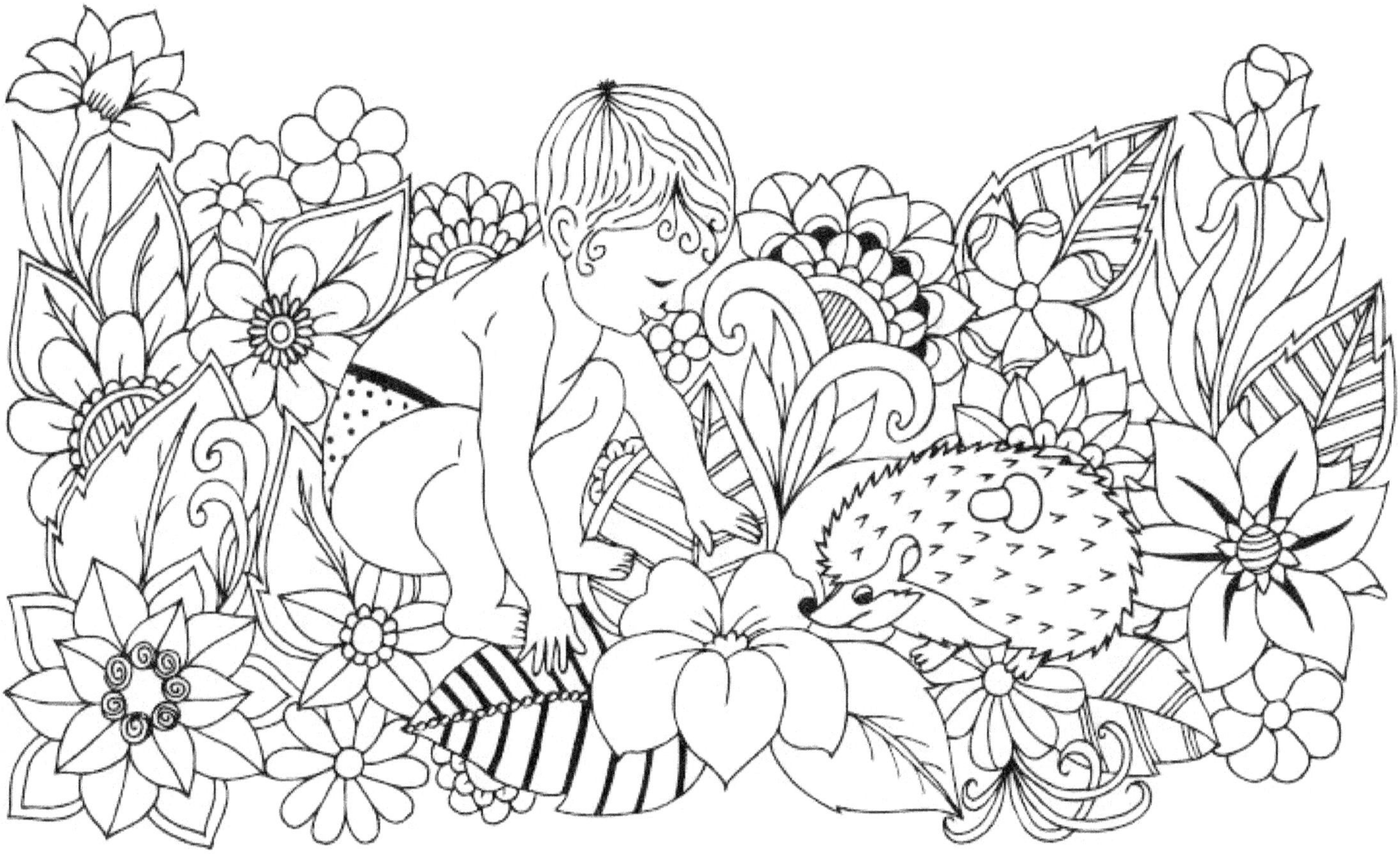

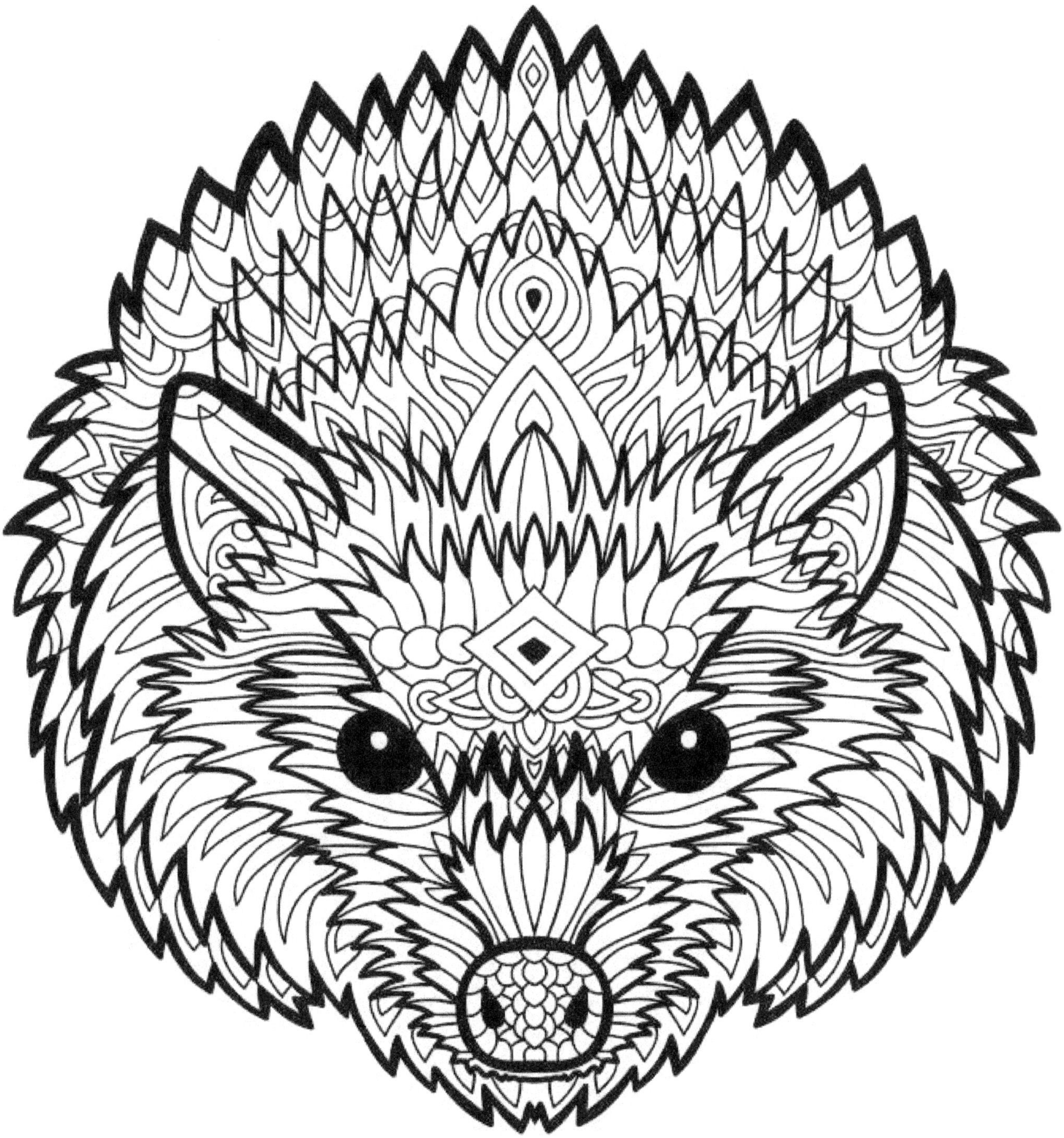

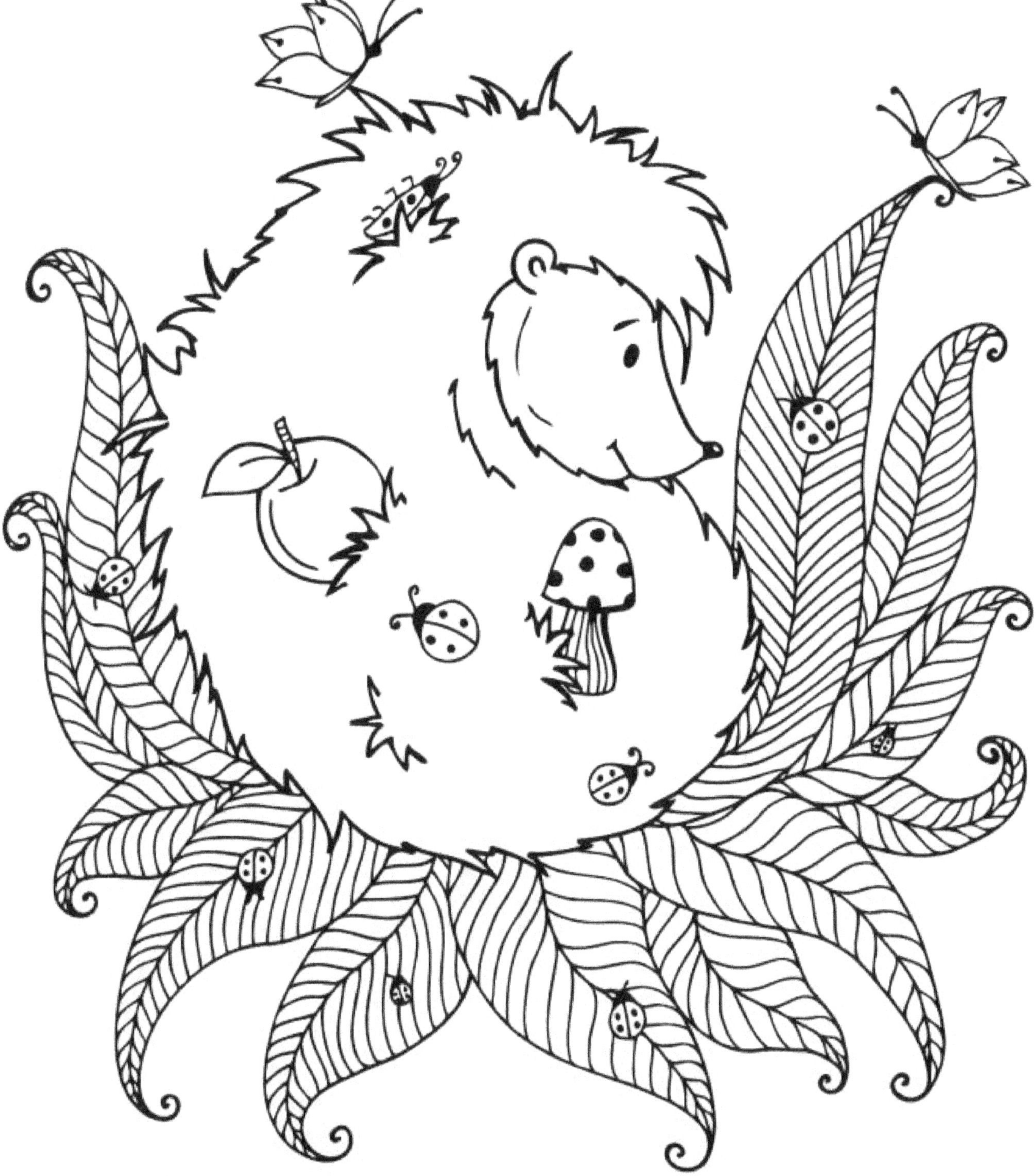

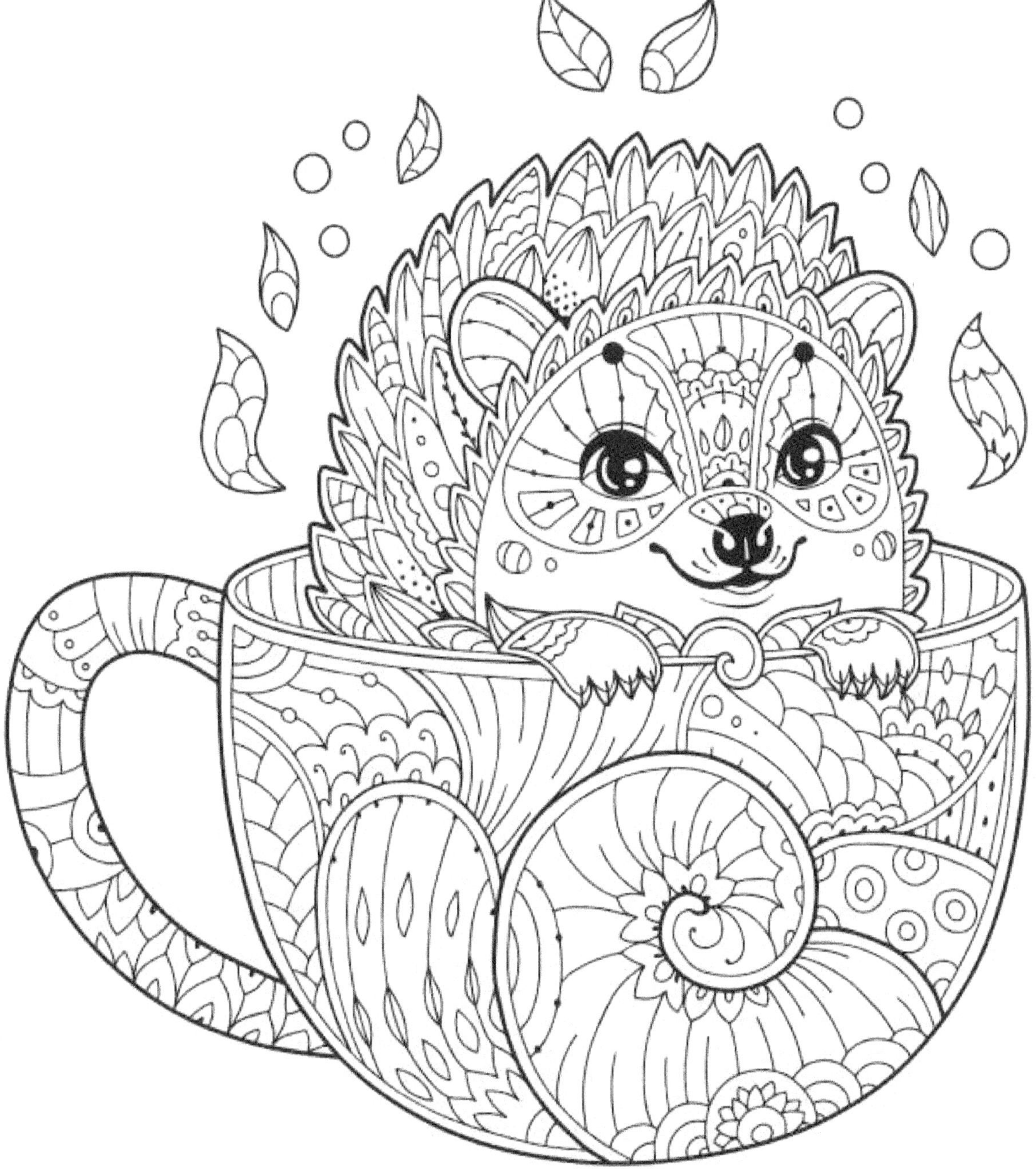

www.ingramcontent.com/pod-product-compliance
Lightning Source LLC
Chambersburg PA
CBHW081756170526
45167CB00009B/4039